A GRAPHIC HISTORY OF THE CIVIL RIGHTS MOVEMENT

THE LITTLE ROCK NINE
AND THE FIGHT FOR EQUAL EDUCATION

BY GARY JEFFREY
ILLUSTRATED BY NANA LI

Gareth Stevens
Publishing

Please visit our website, www.garethstevens.com.
For a free color catalog of all our high-quality books,
call toll free 1-800-542-2595 or fax 1-877-542-2596.

Library of Congress Cataloging-in-Publication Data

Jeffrey, Gary.
The Little Rock nine and the fight for equal education / Gary Jeffrey.
p. cm. — (A graphic history of the civil rights movement)
Includes index.
ISBN 978-1-4339-7484-7 (pbk.)
ISBN 978-1-4339-7485-4 (6-pack)
ISBN 978-1-4339-7483-0 (library binding)
1. School integration—Arkansas—Little Rock—History—20th century—
Juvenile literature. 2. African American students—Arkansas—Little Rock—
History—20th century—Juvenile literature. 3. Central High School (Little
Rock, Ark.)—History—Juvenile literature. 4. Little Rock (Ark.)—Race
relations—Juvenile literature. I. Title.
LC214.23.L56J44 2012
379.2'630976773—dc23
2011045583

First Edition

Published in 2013 by
Gareth Stevens Publishing
111 East 14th Street, Suite 349
New York, NY 10003

Photo credits:
p4-5, Library of Congress; p22b, Steve Snodgrass

Printed in China

CPSIA compliance information: Batch #DWS12GS: For further information contact Gareth Stevens, New York, New York at 1-800-542-2595.

CONTENTS

Since the early 20th century, southern "Jim Crow" laws had kept white and black apart in public. The generally poor quality of colored facilities served to keep African Americans down and remind them of their place. Nowhere was this more obvious than in their schooling.

Although run by dedicated staff, most black-only schools were poorly equipped and shabby compared with white ones.

A BREAKTHROUGH

The National Association for the Advancement of Colored People (NAACP) focused on segregated schools as a way to bring down "Jim Crow." In 1954, they won a landmark decision when the U.S. Supreme Court ruled that segregated schools were unconstitutional. The next challenge would be to get black students actually *attending* white schools.

The NAACP's top lawyer, Thurgood Marshall (center), celebrates the 1954 Brown v. Board of Education decision that rejected the legality of school segregation.

INTEGRATION DRIVE

Little Rock, the state capital of Arkansas, agreed to integrate its schools beginning in 1957. Virgil Blossom, the superintendent of the largest school, Little Rock Central High, asked for a list of possible black students that could be enrolled. Eighty names were put forward.

Blossom knew whoever enrolled would be subject to a rough ride from those opposed to integration. The list was pared down to 32 and then to ten who were thought mentally tough enough to survive the process.

Daisy Bates, who ran a black people's newspaper and was NAACP president in Arkansas, oversaw the enrollment of the Little Rock students.

Confident twelfth-grader Terrence Roberts was the eldest of the group.

Despite a serious heart condition, Thelma Mothershed wanted to become a teacher.

Elizabeth Eckford was a quiet, serious 15-year-old with a passion for rock 'n' roll music.

TEN BRAVE SOULS

They were Ernest Green, Terrence Roberts, Elizabeth Eckford, Minnijean Brown, Thelma Mothershed, Gloria Ray, Melba Pattillo, Jefferson Thomas, Carlotta Walls, and Jane Hill.

Segregationists made it clear they would try and block the ten's school attendance on September 4. State governor Orval Faubus pledged the Arkansas National Guard to keep the peace, but Daisy Bates was still worried. On September 3, she decided the students had better meet up a few blocks from the school and go in together under escort. She managed to tell them all except Elizabeth Eckford, whose family didn't own a phone...

THE LITTLE ROCK NINE AND THE FIGHT FOR EQUAL EDUCATION

IT WAS 8:15 A.M. SEPTEMBER 4, 1957, WHEN ELIZABETH ECKFORD APPROACHED THE MAIN ENTRANCE OF LITTLE ROCK CENTRAL HIGH.

SOLDIERS? MAYBE THEY'RE HERE TO PROTECT ME.

8

MELBA'S MOM THRUST THE CAR KEYS AT MELBA AS THE MOB GOT NEAR.

TAKE THESE! WHATEVER HAPPENS, YOU GET OUT OF HERE! YOU BE SAFE!

MOTHER, I'M NOT LEAVING YOU!

AN ANGRY WHITE MAN PULLED AT LOUISE PATTILLO'S COAT. ANOTHER TRIED TO SWIPE HER WITH A TREE BRANCH.

MELBA STARTED THE CAR AND REVERSED OUT FAST AS HER MOTHER JUMPED IN BESIDE HER.

THEY SPED AWAY JUST IN TIME.

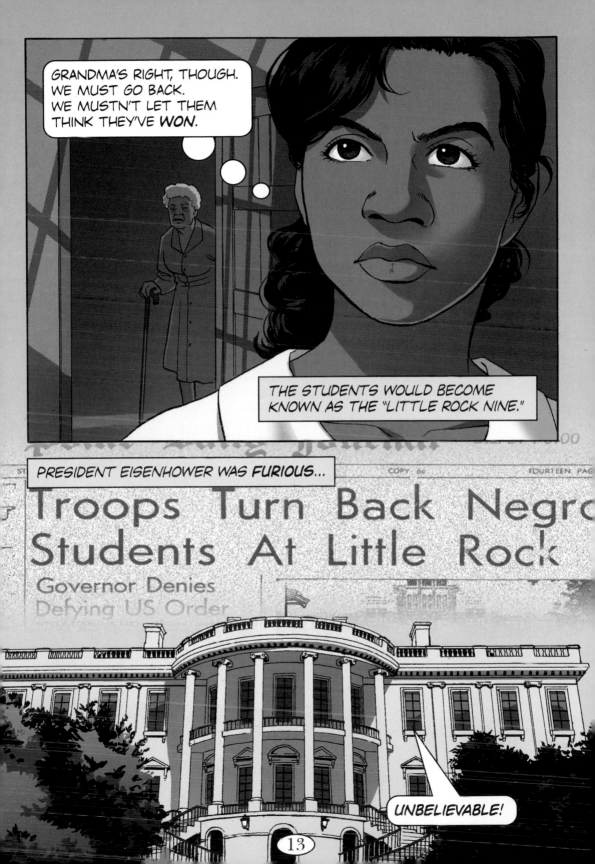

FAUBUS HAS ACTUALLY DEFIED A **FEDERAL ORDER!**

EISENHOWER PRESSURED FAUBUS TO REMOVE THE NATIONAL GUARD.

ON SEPTEMBER 23, TWO POLICE CARS DREW UP TO A SIDE ENTRANCE AT LITTLE ROCK HIGH. AROUND THE CORNER, OVER 1,000 PROTESTERS WERE BARRICADED OUTSIDE THE MAIN ENTRANCE.

TWO, FOUR, SIX, EIGHT, WE AIN'T GONNA INTEGRATE!

15

16

AT THE WHITE HOUSE...

WE CAN'T HAVE MOB RULE.

WELL, THE LITTLE ROCK POLICE AREN'T MUCH HELP. A LOT OF THEM ARE ON THE SIDE OF THE SEGREGATIONISTS!

SEPTEMBER 24, SUMMONED BY THE MAYOR OF LITTLE ROCK, 1,200 U.S. ARMY PARATROOPS LANDED AT LITTLE ROCK AIR BASE.

19

AT 9:25 A.M. WEDNESDAY, SEPTEMBER 25, 1957, THE NINE BLACK STUDENTS WERE FINALLY ADMITTED THROUGH THE FRONT DOORS OF LITTLE ROCK CENTRAL HIGH.

THANK HEAVENS IT'S *OVER*.

THE CONSTITUTIONAL CRISIS WAS OVER, BUT THE *TROUBLE* WAS JUST BEGINNING...

INTO THE CAULDRON

On November 27, the 101st Airborne left Little Rock. Care of the Nine was passed to the newly federalized National Guard and the Nine's rough ride resumed *inside* the school's walls.

SCHOOL OF DISORDER

The Nine had been advised to bear any racist taunts calmly—"like Jackie Robinson." Some found this hard. Minnijean Brown and Jefferson Thomas in particular became the target of abuse. After one fight too many, Minnijean transferred to a school in New York in 1958.

HONORED FOR BRAVERY

Ernest Green became the first to graduate in 1958. All nine went on to become achievers and in 1999 were awarded the Congressional Gold Medal for their bravery in furthering the civil rights cause.

The Nine meet the Mayor of New York in 1958. Minnijean is on the far left.

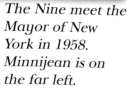

Statues of the Little Rock Nine grace the grounds of the Arkansas State Capitol.

GLOSSARY

barricades Barriers that block off a certain area.

convoy A group of vehicles traveling one after another in a line.

F.B.I. Federal Bureau of Investigation.

"Jim Crow" laws Laws that segregate whites and blacks in public places such as schools.

paratroops Soldiers from the air force who are trained to parachute.

protesters People who speak out against a law or policy in the hope of changing it.

reconstruction The period of rebuilding the South after the Civil War.

ruse A plot or trick intented to deceive someone.

scowling Frowning in disapproval or anger.

segregationists People in favor of keeping blacks and whites separate.

taunts Insulting comments intended to provoke people to respond aggressively.

INDEX